Lighthouses
towers of the sea

Lighthouses
towers of the sea

**Charles Payton, Margaret Willes
and Samantha Wyndham**

 THE NATIONAL TRUST

Introduction

As a child, I was entranced by the New Brighton Lighthouse at the mouth of the Mersey. Visible from Liverpool, and to be visited at low tide by everyone with a bucket and spade, it is a pocket light and could, with a little imagination, be a large model. Arriving on the ferry at New Brighton for a day out on the sands, I suppose the lighthouse stood for comfort and permanence in my childhood mind.

There is a widespread fascination with lighthouses that often has nothing to do with the sea. They stand in the land or seascape as unavoidable structures. Some have great beauty, while others seem to form part of the very elements that they combat. Whatever presence they take, they demand a response from us, which often comes from quite deep within ourselves.

Sooner or later, looking at lighthouses leads to questions about them, and in particular human questions – who, when, where, how and with what? These do not simply extend to their construction, but also to who used and operated them – the mariners and keepers, and their families. Here is the comment of a woman, speaking from first-hand experience:

I hate lighthouses … when a woman marries a lighthouse keeper, she gives up everything else in the world. If I had my life over again, it would not be in lighthouse stations.
Mrs Alexander McLean 1931

And her husband was working not at sea or on the cliffs, but on islands in Lake Michigan!

Something of the black side of this lifestyle is illustrated by the way in which people in cosy homes regarded the lighthouse and its staff. Not that long ago, Christmas-time brought images via newspapers, newsreels and, for a while, television, showing the traditional custom of local inhabitants taking the tree, presents, dinner and supplies to some of the loneliest workplaces on earth, through weather suited only to fish. The bonhomie displayed in the films was, in the style of the newsreaders of the time, a little sugary. But there is no doubt that the coverage reflected the very real gratitude of a nation that understood – a maritime nation in touch with the surrounding sea.

Charles Payton

previous pages: *Harbour Scene - Morning* **painted in 1751 by Joseph Vernet, now at Uppark, West Sussex**

right: New Brighton Lighthouse at the mouth of the River Mersey

Origins

It is not possible to be exact about when someone decided to replace a flickering rush lamp in a window, or a burning brand or beacon on high ground, with a fire upon a tower specifically for a maritime purpose. Some people believe that it was at Sigeum on the southern side of the Hellespont, near Troy, in 660BC.

What we can say with certainty is that the Pharos of Alexandria, at the mouth of the Nile in ancient Egypt, was the world's first true tower lighthouse. Sostratus of Cnidus built it in 300BC and it became one of the ancient wonders of the world, destroyed by an earthquake in the fourteenth century AD. There are strange and probably fanciful illustrations of this light, but we still have no idea of its true structure. Recent finds underwater off Alexandria have pinpointed vast blocks and carvings that may help, but the jury is still out. What we know is that it was a fire set upon a high tower, maintained and visible over many sea miles.

The Romans took to lighthouses with gusto. The Emperor Claudius (who completed the invasion of Britain) built his first around AD42 at the entrance to his new Port of Ostia, the port for Rome. One survives at Boulogne on the north French coast, and Britain has a near complete example at Dover in Kent. This, built in the first century AD, remains as part of the Dover Castle. Another example of a Roman light exists at Corunna on the northern coast of Spain. It was built by the Emperor Trajan in the first century and remains in use, with a modern light chamber on top, as both a light and a radio station.

left: Fanciful depiction of the Pharos of Alexandria in Egypt, painted by Harold Oakley, c.1933

right: The Roman Pharos, to the right of St Mary's Church, at Dover Castle in Kent

Seamarks

Apart from the Roman lighthouse at Dover Castle, early medieval lights were built as parts of monasteries along the south and east coasts of England.

The Benedictine monks of St Michael's Mount in Cornwall built a stone lantern on the corner of a tower, from which they guided fishermen belonging to the island. The lantern was just large enough to admit one person, and it projected perilously above a precipice. It was later known as St Michael's Chair and popular belief had it that if a married woman had the courage to sit in it, she would gain mastery over her husband. Further west on Cape Cornwall was a chapel dedicated to St Nicholas, who doubled as Santa Claus for children and as patron saint of seamen. This chapel, according to John Leland, the Tudor topographer, had a 'pharos for a light for ships sailing by night'. Unusually, this survived the Dissolution, which extinguished so many lights.

Hermits were also medieval lightkeepers. In the reign of Richard II, Brother Matthew erected a beacon on the banks of the Humber on the dangerous east coast. His successor obtained permission from the Crown to exact a toll from every ship entering or leaving the port of Kingston upon Hull, the proceeds

being spent to maintain the light. Within two hundred years, the sea had swept away both hermitage and lighthouse, and despite the hazards of this coast, no light reappeared there until the seventeenth century.

Lights, however, were not the only seamarks used to guide mariners. During the reign of Elizabeth I, an Act was passed in 1566 which refers to the variety of marks that could be used:

Forasmuch as by the destroying and taking away of certain steeples, woods and other marks standing upon the main shores adjoining to the sea coasts of this realm of England and Wales, being as beacons and marks of ancient times accustomed for seafaring men, to save and keep them and the ships in their charge from sundry dangers thereto incident, divers ships with their goods and merchandise in sailing from foreign parts towards this realm of England and Wales, and specially to the port and river of Thames, have by the lack of such marks of late years been miscarried, perished and lost in the sea.

St Michael's Mount in Cornwall: the monks' lantern was mounted at the top of the central church tower

Beacons are connected in our minds with flaming bonfires on high points of land, which can be used as warning devices in times of national danger, such as the approach of the Spanish Armada or Napoleon's threatened invasion of England. However, the term is also used for unlighted pillars and structures set on rocks and sandbanks, especially on the estuaries of rivers. In *Our Seamarks: A plain account of the Lighthouses, Lightships, Beacons, Buoys and Fog-Signals maintained on our Coasts for the Guidance of Mariners*, published in 1884, E. Price Edwards listed 250 recognised beacons on the British coasts. Although very different in style, they all had a special characteristic head to enable mariners to recognise them – a globe, diamond, triangle or cross, for example. Wherever a spot required to be marked, but was not large or important enough to merit the expense of constructing a lighthouse, so one of these beacons was erected.

The Shingles Beacon marked the Shingles Sands off Margate. Erected in the second half of the nineteenth century, it was an iron cylinder, taken out in two pieces. At low water, when the sand was nearly dry, one half of the cylinder was set on the sand. A man then went inside, and dug out the sand, sending it up in buckets. As the sand was removed, so the cylinder sank, aided by battering until it was fifteen feet down. The other half was then fastened onto it, and the operation continued until it was set twenty-five feet into the sand. The inside was then filled up with shingle mixed with cement. A diamond-shaped frame was set on top of the cylinder.

Also in Kent was the beacon for Goodwin Sands. This was erected in the 1840s, with an iron mast and ladder steps leading up to a refuge cage, where several people could huddle well above the highwater mark. This was swept away on this notorious site *(see page 54)* in 1877.

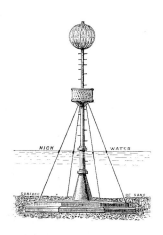

above: The Goodwin Beacon, built in the 1840s on the Goodwin Sands in Kent, from E. Price Edwards, *Our Seamarks ...*

right: Beacons lit on the headlands of the National Trust's Golden Cap Estate in Dorset, to commemorate the 400th anniversary of the arrival of the Spanish Armada in 1588

Henry VIII grants the first Charter to the Trinity House: MDXIV

List of Benefactors of the Corporation of Trinity House, London, transcribed in the year MCMXXVI from the tablets hitherto affixed to the South Wall of the Quarter Deck in their House on Gower Hill, with additions

Gemulas in Unitate

Trinity House

As we have seen, medieval lights were usually maintained by monks and hermits.

But others were built and looked after by mariners and pilots who formed themselves into guilds or trade associations called Trinity Houses. Trinity Houses are known to have existed in at least seven ports, including Dundee and Leith in Scotland, Newcastle upon Tyne and Kingston upon Hull, and in London, based at Deptford on the south bank of the Thames, a couple of miles downstream from London Bridge. The London Trinity House was linked with Deptford parish church, which was dedicated to St Clement, an early Christian who suffered martyrdom by being thrown into the sea weighted down by an anchor.

Henry VIII, as in so many aspects of English history, made an interesting contribution to lighthouses. In the 1530s, his Dissolution of the Monasteries put paid to many of the early lights, but he also established the first standing navy and granted Trinity House its charter of incorporation on 20 May 1514, which ensured the continuing development of lighthouses.

The charter refers to 'our trewe and faithfull subjects, shipmen and mariners … to begyn of new and erect and establish a Guild or Brotherhood of themselves or other persons as well men as women, whatsoever they be'. It is remarkable that women were included in an activity which might be regarded as an exclusively male domain. This charter was confirmed by Charles II after the Restoration of the monarchy. Later modifications under successive monarchs decreed that there should be 'Elder Brethren' to assist the master and wardens, and allowed 'Younger Brethren' to be elected but to remain at sea as associates. This structure survives to this day, with HRH Prince Philip, Duke of Edinburgh, as Master, and experienced sea officers in the Royal Navy and the Merchant Service as Younger Brethren.

An illuminated page from the Benefactors' Roll showing King Henry VIII granting the charter to Trinity House

The leading authority on lighthouses worldwide, Trinity House has automated all its lights and concentrates on modern technology (solar power, satellite navigation, telemetry and digital signalling) for its operations. Recognising the need to engage the public more closely in its works, it offers passage aboard a fine maintenance ship, *Patricia*, with visits to ten working lighthouses.

Lighthouses were and are expensive, highly sophisticated buildings to create and to maintain. Since Henry VIII's charter of 1514, Trinity House has subsequently become the General Lighthouse Authority for England, Wales, the Channel Islands and Gibraltar. But this did not spell the end of private enterprise, using the income from 'dues'. These were charges levied from the thirteenth century onwards on ships navigating relevant waters, collected by customs officers on behalf of the Crown. Needless to say, much dishonesty and fraud went on because the dues added up to huge sums and therefore offered attractive pickings.

Trinity House ran into financial difficulties early in its existence, but in 1594 the Lord High Admiral of England, Lord Howard of Effingham, gave up his traditional rights to the 'perks' obtained from selling ballast to ships unloading their cargoes in the port of London. This revenue was diverted to Trinity House, which took over the responsibility for dredging shingle from the Thames and selling it to masters of ships in need of ballast. The money helped the organisation to begin building lighthouses that were badly needed along the east coast to protect merchant ships engaged in the coal trade between Newcastle and London. To maintain these lighthouses, a levy of twelve pence per ton was imposed on all ships sailing from the ports of Newcastle, Hull, Boston and King's Lynn.

Lights, however, continued to be built under patent permissions from the Crown, which were then owned and operated by individuals. The profits from dues were so astronomical that this practice continued until the government finally took action in 1836. The resulting Act of Parliament empowered Trinity House to buy out all the lighthouses in private hands. The last to be purchased was Skerries Rock, off Anglesey in North Wales, which was acquired in 1841 after a stiff tussle.

The patent to build Skerries was granted on 13 July 1714 to William Tench. He was also granted the right to collect, from all shipping that passed the rock, a compulsory levy of one penny per ship and twopence per ton of cargo for the upkeep of the light. The lease was originally for sixty years at an annual rent of £5 to the Crown. By the time Trinity House sought to buy the lighthouse, the then owner, Morgan Jones, was enjoying the most profitable lighthouse on the coasts of England and Wales, and rejected the astronomical figure of £399,500. When Trinity House asked him for his own estimate of the compensation owed to him, he refused to give a figure, and the case went to court. In the words of the Lighthouse Society of Great Britain, 'In his greedy manipulation of human justice, he did not bargain for natural justice, which caused him to die in March 1841 before the final negotiations were completed.' This took place the following July, when the jury awarded his heir £444,984 in compensation (£15 million in today's figures).

THV Patricia, the flagship of the Trinity House fleet, on which passengers can cruise while she undertakes her maintenance duties

The Light

Living as we do with profound light pollution everywhere, it is hard to understand how a faint light can be seen over miles of darkened sea. Most of us have no idea what real darkness is, at least in the open air. Try, however, using something tiny for light in a completely blacked-out room – maybe a mobile phone with a flashing indicator or a screen that lights up; maybe the tiny diode on a television or radio. Once you have allowed your eyes to adapt, and it takes quite a time for many (typically about four minutes), the light becomes something significant, easily seen, and in the imagination much bigger than it actually is, *particularly if it flashes*. Darkness that is split by even a small spark makes its light extraordinarily powerful.

Your brain is programmed to use your eyes to detect minuscule movements and every photon of light that it can. Your survival as a species depends upon that ability. It is the same talent that allows you to see a face in a crowd, a lone pigeon moving on a crowded railway concourse, or the single ear of a roving deer in a cornfield. You react either to hunt or to fly. So a light exposed in darkness at sea, once your night vision is in place, is always an immediate call to attention, however small it may be. The human eye even sees the trail left by a fish fin dragging phosphorescence. It's all down to that old matter of movement and light.

A lighthouse is either tall or is located high up, although this can be overdone as at the Old Lundy Light *(see pp.76-77)*. Elevation of the light is essential to its long-distance visibility. It is reckoned that, when your eye is eight feet above the surface of the sea, your horizon is around three nautical miles away. As you get higher, so your vision extends.

In calculating lighthouse visibility, it is generally assumed that the minimum height of the viewer is fifteen feet above the water, giving an horizon of about four-and-a-half nautical miles. Now, for those with mathematical minds, the further advantage of a light set at a great height above the sea will become obvious. In fact, the lighthouse will be seen before you would predict, because refraction and the curvature of the earth will make it visible actually *over the horizon that is yours*.

Souter Lighthouse, Tyne & Wear, illuminated at dusk

The Lens

The problem that remains, however, is that light decays as distance increases from the source, so that simply putting it high up is not enough. Yes, a candle can be spied a long way off in profound darkness, but if the mariner is really to be helped, the output of the lamp must be increased. This was only made possible by enclosing the source of light within a clear glass lantern. Once protected, glass was used again to improve the visibility, by creating lenses which magnified, concentrated and directed the light.

Early lights were static. They did not flash and the candles within hung in large candelabra, sending light all round, or in one direction if part of the lantern was blanked out. This light was pure or unconcentrated. However, once oil was used to produce light, it rapidly became obvious that the flame would benefit from some sort of focus to make all the photons shine together in one place.

First came dished reflectors, followed by the parabolic variety. The latter has the property of taking in the reflected light from the whole lamp and from all directions, and sending it out in a cone. We see this every day in car headlights and torches. Lamps like this are called catoptric, and can be either static or, where motion is required, several can be mounted around a frame and then revolved to show flashes of light.

During the seventeenth and eighteenth centuries, scientists became fascinated with light, resulting in the vital discovery that light bends when it passes through various materials, as in the case of water, where what you see through from the surface is displaced from its true position. The developers of lights for lighthouses took advantage of this principle by using prisms surrounding lenses, which received the light from behind and then sent it out in straight lines once again. This system of refraction is called dioptric. In time, the two systems – the reflector behind the light and the refraction before it – were combined into a catadioptric system to produce the wonderful sculpted glass of the lighthouse lamp, a remarkable meeting of art and science.

These lamps and optics were and are extremely heavy, but a way was found to revolve them by floating them upon a liquid; one man in ideal conditions can actually move a large ship. To float the entire lamp was the key, but it could not be done on water because the resulting tower would have to be vast in order to contain enough water at the top to support tons of lamp.

The solution was ingenious. Mercury supports 35 times more weight by volume than water. Arrays of catadioptrics could now be mounted on frames and revolved around a static lamp. Tons in weight floating on these mercury baths can literally be turned with a little finger, and so mechanisms to drive them were at first no different from large clocks and, later, small electric motors. Both can be seen in operation today.

The lenses at Souter Lighthouse

The Power

The lamp at the heart of the lighthouse has undergone significant changes. The Eddystone Lighthouse built by John Smeaton in the mid-eighteenth century had a light of 24 candles *(see p.26)*. This may seem puny, but the lens made it possible to see this light through a telescope 12 nautical miles away. When very high-quality spermaceti candles arrived, it became possible to establish a new standard. These candles, made from a waxy substance obtained from sperm whales, gave off a very bright, predictable and steady level of light that could be accurately measured. Even today, we refer to light values in terms of 'candle power' from the sperm whale's superb candles.

Candles gave way to oil, because obviously it was easier to keep a tank topped up and burning than constantly replacing the candles. Again, the very best of these lights connects with the old whaling days – but *not* the blubber whales of the northern oceans, whose product stank, smoked and was poor in quality. Only one whale mattered, the whale of Moby Dick, the sperm whale. Hunters of the sperm whale produced, in a deeply hazardous trade, two main resources: head matter or spermaceti, an odourless wax (from which the candles came); and boiled-down body blubber which produced the finest 'oil' known. This does not rot, is sweet to the smell and is of very high quality. These products were not synthesised

or replaceable in their many uses until after the Second World War.

By the end of the eighteenth century, the lights available were so good that improvements in lenses and in mechanisms became the priority. A Swiss physicist and chemist, Aimé Argand, brought the next change. Oil lights had been in use for some time, but in 1793 he invented a burner that gave an all-through and all-round controlled draught to the flame, thus producing a bright and steady light for the first time. Technical refinements and price rises in sperm oil resulted in the introduction of other vegetable and aromatic oils. Oil remained in use until late in the nineteenth century, and pressurised paraffin continued to be used into the twentieth century.

Generators and pressurised air tanks at Souter Lighthouse

Gas

Town gas obtained from coal was used to light city streets from the early 1800s, but the manufacture of gas required large-scale premises and involved much pollution, making it unsuitable for remote lighthouses. One gas did emerge, however, that was simple to produce and easy to use, although it was hugely explosive. Acetylene gas, produced by reacting carbide and water, was also easy to transport. Moreover, it produces a blindingly powerful light, as you will know if you have ever unwisely watched an acetylene welder at work.

Acetylene proved so successful that it continued to be used in lighthouses right up to the closing years of the twentieth century. At first, it was generated in plants at the light, as in the Farne Islands, where the generator house can still be seen and the nearby cliff has been stained white by the slaked lime thrown out as a waste product (see p.36-37). Latterly, it came in bottled form, as at Foula in the Orkneys, which was built in 1986 and gas-powered until 2000 when it was converted to solar/wind power.

A strange connection exists between this gas, the sun and a kitchen cooker. Acetylene can be very reliable, and therefore seemed ideal for automatic lights and beacons. But in order to make it

work in this way, a valve had to be invented that was powered by the sun, so that the generation of the gas could be turned on at night and off in the day. The man who achieved this was Gustav Dalen, a prolific Swedish inventor and recipient of the Nobel Prize for Physics in 1912, who devised a way to store acetylene under high pressure in acetone. One experiment too far took his eyesight in an explosion, but he never stopped working. In 1929, he invented the famous AGA cooker to help his wife in the kitchen, the idea for which came from his experiments in thermal technics.

Electricity

Michael Faraday, the father of electricity, was born in 1791 at Newington Butts in south London. By coincidence, he grew up near one of the most productive spermaceti presses, established within easy reach of Price's famous candle works at Battersea. By 1821, he had discovered electro-magnetic rotation – the principle behind the electric motor – and, ten years later, electro-magnetic induction, which led to transformers and generators. Demonstrating innovatory vision, Trinity House appointed him Scientific Adviser only five years later in 1836.

Faraday set about improving and refining oil lights. In the 1840s, he

invented a more efficient chimney for the lamps, thus removing the sooty deposits that fogged up the lantern windows and were the bane of the lighthouse keeper. This was patented by his brother Robert, and installed in all lighthouses. A decade later, he was hard at work on ways and means of bringing electric light to the system. This pace of development is similar to the advances made towards airborne flight in the twentieth century, and was just as spectacular.

Faraday's discovery of electrical induction was carried further by others. Perhaps the most important developments took place in France. In 1852, an Anglo-French business successfully produced a Faraday generator with enough power to support a light. This steam-powered generator, refined and developed by Faraday and his associate, Professor F.H. Holmes, was used to produce intense light by passing a current across the space between two 'pencils' of carbon. Faraday was delighted with the power, simplicity and manageability of the carbon arc light, and it was installed and tested in the Dungeness and South Foreland lighthouses in Kent. In December 1858, the world's first seawards electric lamp was installed at South Foreland (see p.58). But, like any new technology, the Holmes generator was hugely expensive, and refinement and redevelopment followed. At last, in 1870, it was installed in the purpose-built Souter Lighthouse between the Tyne and the Wear *(see p.43)*, thus beginning the deployment of electric power throughout the Trinity House lighthouses.

It remained only for the coming of efficient incandescent bulbs shortly afterwards for the light quality of today to be achieved. All this had happened in the astonishingly short time of 50 years, from a standing start. Faraday was born into the light of candles and died in the flood of limelight. Right to the present day, however, and even through the continuous development of increasingly powerful bulbs, a link has been maintained with the earlier history of the modern light. In order to guard against breakdown, almost every lighthouse has lights installed on triangular bases containing two electric bulbs, along with either gas or oil lights so that an alternative is always available.

**Michael Faraday; photograph by
Maull & Polyblank, 1857**

Fog

Even a hugely powerful light only penetrates fog for a short distance. Every droplet of water and particle of matter bounces it all over the place. The blanket also muffles, and if you have been in a profound fog, you will remember not just blindness but a curious silence, again caused by the myriad droplets absorbing sound.

So what to do? The solution lies in very loud noise, preferably directed and concentrated. Early attempts involved bells, but many a ship never heard them. Cannon were used and the roar of a gun at a particularly hazardous site was, for decades, the best man could devise. This sound was focused by the barrel and did, in fact, penetrate to a considerable distance. If it did not have much directional capability, at least the mazed sailor out at sea could hear something was up and take precautions.

As the eighteenth century drew to a close, steam power began to be understood and this new source of energy was developed rapidly.

The fog signal station at Souter Lighthouse

It was not long before steam provided a new way of warning in fog. Strange that a problem of water droplets should be tackled with water vapour. Robert Foulis (pronounced Fowles) was probably the first man to twig that a whistle blown by steam would be an improvement, particularly if it blew to a pattern of blasts and intensities. Foulis was born in Glasgow in 1796, but emigrated to North America, landing in Halifax, Nova Scotia, in 1818. Having moved in 1821 to Saint John in New Brunswick, Canada, he was appointed deputy land surveyor for the province, and began to work on steamboat navigation, which gave him a taste for maritime matters. One of his achievements was to install gas lighting in a lighthouse on Partridge Island, at the mouth of Saint John harbour, where both cannon and a huge bell had failed as fog warnings, at great cost. Foulis realised that a whistle blown by steam would be more effective, and duly presented plans to the Commissioners of Lights in 1852 and again in 1858. His second set of plans were stolen by Vernon Smith, who made minor alterations, submitted them successfully to the Commissioners, and subsequently built the world's first steam fog alarm on Partridge Island in 1859. It continued in operation until it was shut down in 1998. Foulis was eventually credited with the invention in 1864, but he received no financial benefit because an almost identical steam fog whistle had by then been patented in the USA. He died in poverty at Saint John in 1866.

The next great advance in fog warning has yet another whimsical connection. During the 1890s, Robert Hope-Jones, chief electrician of the Lancashire and Cheshire Telephone Company, took out a series of patents on the application of low voltage electrical currents to church organs. Amongst these, in 1897, was Patent Number 21,389 for an organ stop converted into a foghorn – the diaphone which is still used in lighthouses today.

Using very simple components, it produces a tuneable and deafening resonance from compressed air, blown through something that is essentially similar to the reed pipe of an organ. In order to run it, steam plants and, later, motors were installed to work a compressor that stored air in accumulators. Vast and often rather beautiful horns attached to this apparatus produce a noise that can be heard for miles. These can be customised to ensure that they are not confused with other foghorns. A good example of the entire mechanism can be seen at Souter Lighthouse *(see p.44)*.

Hope-Jones's revolutionary work on organs resulted in the electro-pneumatic action that meant keyboards could be sited anywhere, rather than being tied to the pipe-case itself. In 1903, he suddenly packed his bags and emigrated to America, where he eventually sold all his patents, name and goodwill to the Wurlitzer Company. The mighty Wurlitzer Theatre Organ contains powerful stops on the diaphone principle.

Building Lighthouses

Lighthouses consisted initially of platforms, followed by towers of one kind or another. The earliest Greek and Roman towers were mostly built with ragstone cores, over which a facing, such as dressed stone, was laid. The Roman lighthouse at Dover Castle shows this form of structure laid bare *(see p.7)*. These, and the later land towers, followed well-tried building principles of their time, and incorporated the local materials of their situation.

However, once the light was carried out to sea, by whatever distance, a huge leap in technology was required. Maritime building is a terribly difficult thing to accomplish. The sea is mistress of it all. Even erecting beacons using iron posts set into the rocks with molten lead, or putting up iron structures for the same purpose, was fraught with difficulties. Imagine sailing to the rock in a small boat, with only pickaxes, chisels, shovels, rope and tackle to help you when you get there. Explosives are denied you,

because in many cases you cannot risk damaging the rocks you want to use as foundations. Shelter is absent and the tide will allow you only a few hours of work, even on the finest of days. It is sobering to note that, in early attempts, only a few days' or weeks' work was accomplished in periods of construction lasting many years. And at the end of it, the enormous energy of the waves could wipe away the beacon, and the memory of all that arduous work, in just one winter.

The first attempt to build a permanent offshore light was made by the eccentric artist, inventor and shipowner, Henry Winstanley. Having lost ships on the savage rocks of the Eddystone reef, 14 miles off Plymouth in Devon, he constructed a wooden tower on top of a five-metre-high masonry drum. The work took more than two years, and at one point Winstanley was captured by a passing French privateer, but he was finally able to light the candelabra in November

1698. Sadly, he also foreshadowed the continuing hazard of building and operating lighthouses, for while trying to demonstrate his absolute confidence in its construction, he died when his lighthouse was washed away in the Great Storm of 1703 – a tempest stronger even than our hurricane of 1987.

Six years later, the first successful wooden tower – the second Eddystone Lighthouse – was completed by John Rudyerd. A conical structure, it remained undefeated by the sea for 46 years, but finally perished in a dramatic fire in 1755, thus making way for the first real advance in construction, this time in stone. The Plymouth Superintendent, while investigating the fire, pondered: 'Whether this Accident proceeded from their [the keepers] Drinking too much of three Pints of Gin received with the Provisions and Candles that Evening, or having too great a fire in the chimney I cannot discover, but must observe at the time the Fire was discovered that there was but one Bucket in the [light] House.'

The third Eddystone Lighthouse was built by John Smeaton, a Fellow of the Royal Society who is known as the father of English civil engineering. In 1756, he was 31 years old, with a background in the disciplines of science and engineering, but he also brought nature to the Eddystone. What was needed, he said, was to copy the oak tree by constructing a stone tower with a broad base tapering inwards towards the top. His lighthouse was built in granite blocks, each of which was dovetailed to its neighbour to provide added strength. Vertically, these layers were also locked together with tree nails. These tapered oak wedges, long used in wooden shipbuilding, were rounded pins that could be driven into and expanded in a hole between the two sections to be fastened together. In order to bond the many layers, Smeaton invented a quick-drying cement called hydraulic lime, which could resist the action of seawater.

Henry Winstanley's Eddystone Lighthouse, from John Smeaton's *A Narrative of the Building of the Edystone Light,* **1791**

Smeaton's workforce of tough Cornish tin miners built the light in just over three years, bringing it into operation in October 1759. So successful was the construction that the light stayed working for 120 years, until it was forced to close in 1879 because the rock upon which it stood was cracking. In 1882, as a memorial to Smeaton, his Eddystone Lighthouse was dismantled stone by stone, leaving behind the stump of its base. Transported to the mainland, it was re-erected on Plymouth Hoe, where it can be inspected as the first-ever successful stone marine lighthouse.

If the Eddystone, exposed to Atlantic rollers 14 miles off Plymouth, presented difficulties overcome by Smeaton, then Bell Rock was an order of a different magnitude. Again, it is 14 miles out to sea, off the Firth of Tay in Scotland, but it is located in an area where even modern oil rigs suffer some of the worst weather in the world. For centuries, men tried to establish a warning on Bell Rock, but all to no avail. The man who succeeded was Robert Stevenson, the father of a dynasty of lighthouse builders and grandfather of the famous writer, Robert Louis Stevenson.

Following the demise of the 64-gun warship *H.M.S. York* on the Bell Rock in 1804, with the loss of all 491 people on board, the Northern Lighthouse Board appointed Britain's most eminent engineer, John Rennie, to give advice. He revisited a plan, first submitted by Stevenson in 1800, for a 100-foot-high tower on Bell Rock, and was duly appointed Chief Engineer with Stevenson as his assistant, responsible for the on-site erection of the building.

Rennie and Stevenson both acknowledged that the new light would have to be built using the pioneering work of Smeaton at the Eddystone. Rennie widened the curve of the base to withstand the North Sea and ordered an increase in the dovetailing. But the credit for the remainder of this astonishing achievement must go to Stevenson. As Bell Rock is submerged on every tide, the men were only able to work for a maximum of five hours during the calmest days of summer. Construction began in 1807, with the erection of a wooden work tower on legs and the installation of a special iron crane that would eventually lift

the one-ton sculpted stone pieces of the tower. The Bell Rock Lighthouse was completed four years later, in 1811, a marvel of interlocking blocks held together with tree nails and vertical stone wedges, but with no cement in the entire structure. It is still standing today, and remains a working lighthouse nearly 200 years after its construction.

James Douglass, Engineer-in-Chief to Trinity House, brought an added refinement to the work of Robert Stevenson and his son Alan, who had further developed the method of interlocking stone blocks. Rather than pinning the layers of stones, Douglass suggested that they should be dovetailed vertically as well as horizontally, thus in effect creating a single man-made rock of the base and walls. He first used this technique in the construction of the Les Hanois Lighthouse, off the coast of Guernsey, and then, during the 1860s, in the hazardous building of the Wolf Rock Lighthouse, ten miles south-west of Land's End. Douglass also built Souter Lighthouse, which was completed in 1871 *(see pp.42-43)*, and – most famously – the fourth and present Eddystone Lighthouse, thought to be as strong as a natural

granite massif. It stands as a lasting monument to the ingenuity of English and Scottish engineers and scientists, who led the world in the development of offshore lights.

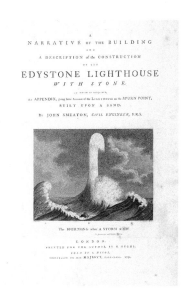

left: John Smeaton's Eddystone Lighthouse, completed in 1759, from an engraving in his book, *A Narrative of the Building of the Edystone Light*, 1791

above: The title-page of John Smeaton's *A Narrative of the Building of the Edystone Light*, showing high seas breaking over the Eddystone Lighthouse

The Lighthouse Keeper

In 1998, the last six keepers departed from the lighthouse at North Foreland in Kent, ending four centuries of tradition. The life they had just left behind was a particular one, requiring all kinds of special qualities and a certain kind of character. This is well summed up by a piece from the *Cornhill Magazine*, dating from 1875:

Whatever else happens, he [the lighthouse keeper] is to do this. He may be isolated through the long night-watches, twenty miles from land, fifty or a hundred feet above the level of the sea, with the winds and waves howling round him, and the sea-birds dashing themselves to death against the gleaming lantern, like giant moths against a candle; or it may be a calm, voluptuous, moonlight night, the soft air laden with the perfumes of the Highland heather or the Cornish gorse, tempting him to keep his watch outside the lantern, in the open gallery, instead of in the watch-room chair within; the Channel may be full of stately ships, each guided by his light; or the horizon may be bare of all signs of life, except, remote and far beneath him, the lantern of some fishing-boat at sea; but whatever may be going on outside, there is within him the duty, simple and easy, by virtue of his moral method and orderly training, 'to light the lamps every evening at sun-setting, and keep them constantly burning, bright and clear, till sun-rising'.

In the late nineteenth century, men entering the service had to be under 28 years of age. They would spend the first year or two learning how to manage and look after the very elaborate apparatus, as well as training to be competent carpenters and plumbers. From the central Trinity House depot at Harwich in Essex, they would be sent out to undertake temporary duties at different lighthouses, under the title of Supernumerary Assistant Keepers. Once they had served this apprenticeship, they were promoted to Assistant Keepers and, in due course, through ability and appropriate conduct, became Principal Keepers. All keepers were required to take their turn on the isolated rock stations, though veterans were usually placed in the more comfortable shore stations.

There would usually be four keepers for an offshore rock lighthouse: three present, and one at leave on shore. Each keeper had to remain on duty at the lighthouse for two consecutive months, followed by a month's holiday on the mainland. This arrangement was not required on land stations, where the keepers could live with their families in cottages alongside the lighthouse, as at Souter *(see p.47)*. Occasionally, whole families inhabited offshore stations, as was the case with the Darling family, including Grace and her mother, who lived on the Longstone Rock Lighthouse off the Farne Islands *(see p.40-41)*.

Supervision of keepers was careful and constant. Official inspectors would undertake their tours by ship during the night, checking to see that the lights were correct, and if necessary landing and gaining admittance with a key. Coastguards were instructed to report any lights that failed or were extinguished, and masters of passing vessels also had more than a passing interest in ensuring that everything was working to order.

The Principal Keeper at Strumble Head Lighthouse in Wales, instructing his Assistant Keepers on the observation of ships offshore in about 1960

Life on rock lighthouses was very different from that on land stations. In the latter, a keeper could lead a fairly conventional life with his family in their cottage, with a garden and a piggery. Men based on rock lighthouses out at sea had a much more constrained existence. Space was limited, with walking exercise mostly confined to the gallery outside the lantern. The authorities made sure that they had plenty to do to occupy their time, with weather reports, daily journals and expenditure accounts to write up, and apparatus to clean. Look-out was maintained both day and night. When time allowed, men would catch a few fish from the rocks. Bell Rock Lighthouse, off the Firth of Tay, boasted a library. This way of life pertained, with relatively few changes, right through the twentieth century until the automation of lighthouses.

The extraordinary life of a keeper on a rock lighthouse attracted some strange characters. The lighthouse builder, John Smeaton, recalled a shoemaker who entered the Eddystone Lighthouse off Plymouth because he longed for a solitary life and found himself less a prisoner there than in his close and confined workshop. When some of his friends expressed astonishment at his choice, he replied: 'Each to his taste. I have always been partial to independence.'

Perhaps he was the same individual who, having served at the Eddystone for nearly 14 years, conceived such an attachment to the place that he gave up his turn of leave. Finally persuaded to go ashore, he found himself 'out of his element' and, contradicting his previous record of quiet and orderly behaviour, drank until he was completely intoxicated. He was carried back to the Eddystone insensible, where, after languishing for a few days, he expired.

Over a mile from Land's End in Cornwall, the first Longships Lighthouse was built on the granite islet of Carn Bras in 1795. Although the rock rose 45 feet above the water, in winter gales both the rock and the lighthouse could be momentarily covered by gigantic waves. They were even known to surmount the lantern, and on one occasion broke the glass and extinguished the light.

One day in 1862, two black flags floated above the summit of the tower. Of the three men who inhabited the tower, the one keeping watch appeared to have thrust a knife into his breast. His companions tried to staunch the blood by plugging the wound with bits of tow. Three days later, their distress signal was seen, but the seas were so rough that the wounded man had to be lowered into a boat suspended in a makeshift crane. He died a few days later after reaching shore, and the jury, acting upon the evidence of his companions, declared that he had committed suicide under an attack of temporary insanity.

A motor launch from the Trinity House maintenance vessel *THV Satellite*, winching a keeper off the Eddystone Lighthouse in about 1950

Types and Locations

There are three basic locations for lighthouses. The most ancient positions are on high or low land, and are situated above harbour entrances or hazardous approaches. Most of the lighthouses owned by the National Trust are of this type. They are often accompanied by an extensive range of outbuildings for accommodation, power, radio facilities and foghorns. Lights like these have a look of great permanence, and indeed are often solidly part of the landscape. But there are exceptions: the 'walking' lighthouses of Dungeness in Kent, for example. Here, because of the movement of the coastline, several lighthouses have been built, each one further to the east. Today you can see them standing within sight of each other.

Secondly, there are the lighthouses located on the inter-tidal shore or on the beach. These are often structures built on legs, resembling a section of a pier on iron supports, with a small wooden building on top. They are often strangely attractive, in a Heath Robinson sort of way, and occasionally they are very beautiful. The lighthouse at Burnham-on-Sea in Somerset is stunning, not only for itself, but also for its setting.

Finally, there are the towers of the sea. Sometimes these are close in to the shore, as at Beachy Head in Sussex, but often they are to be glimpsed over the horizon. If you want to see a truly riotous assembly of lighthouses, including land-based buildings, shore-line structures and deep-sea towers, check out the northern coast of Brittany in France, which has more per square kilometre than anywhere else on earth.

In the following pages are the stories of the lighthouses owned by the National Trust, together with accounts of those that stand on land owned by the Trust but which are still maintained and run by Trinity House.

left: Beachy Head Lighthouse in East Sussex

right: The lighthouse at Burnham-on-Sea in Somerset

The Farne Islands

The Farne Islands lie in the North Sea, between one and five miles off the Northumberland coast. There are approximately fifteen to thirty separate islands, depending on the state of the tide. These are home to a range of seabirds: fifteen species nest here regularly, including terns, guillemots, puffins and the eider duck. The National Trust has owned the Farne Islands since 1925, and runs the whole property as an internationally famous nature reserve.

A swift glance at a map will show the extreme hazard posed by these islands, lying, as they do, across the coastline routes and ever ready to catch any unfortunate vessels blown ashore. It is therefore not surprising that the idea of lights for shipping here is very old. In AD635, St Aidan founded a community of monks on Holy Island, and St Cuthbert lived for several years as a hermit on Inner Farne, where he died in 687. Viking raids drove the monks from the islands in 875, but within two centuries they had been re-established by the Benedictine priory of Lindisfarne. We do not know whether the monks kept a light to warn ships, but the tower they built in about 1500, named after Prior Castell, was later used as a beacon.

The rocks of Staple Island with the Longstone Lighthouse on the horizon

In 1673 it was converted into a lighthouse by Sir John Clayton, who added iron baskets on the top to burn wood or coal every night. However, it appears that this was never lit, because Sir John was unable to gain approval from Trinity House and also failed to persuade Newcastle shipowners to pay him any dues.

By 1776, the need to alert shipping to the presence of the islands and the treacherous tides that swept around them had become desperately serious. Trinity House granted a lease to the Blackett family, the then owners of the islands, for the construction of two lighthouses, one on Inner Farne and the second on Staple Island, both of which were lit in September 1778. Eighteen years later, in 1796, Robert Darling and his family moved into a third new lighthouse on Brownsman's Island.

However, the lighthouse on Staple Island was repeatedly damaged by severe weather, and shipmasters complained about the efficacy of the fixed light on Brownsman's.

Finally, in 1810, Trinity House commissioned Daniel Alexander to build a lighthouse on Inner Farne, in a strikingly beautiful cliff-top location. It is this light that is seen from the mainland, surrounded by later additions and modifications. Built originally as an oil lamp, it progressed to acetylene gas in 1910, when the generator house was constructed to convert carbide to gas. Over the years, the waste product from this process gradually whitened the cliffs below the lighthouse. Today, it is powered by solar-charged batteries and is, like all other functioning lights, uninhabited and controlled by Trinity House from Harwich.

Further out in the Farne Islands, Alexander also built a second lighthouse on the Outer Farne, or Longstone. Erected on a reef, it is a dramatic example of the tower in the sea. Robert Darling was transferred there as the new keeper, and it was later taken over by his son William, who lived there with his family, including his daughter Grace. While the life of a keeper was hard, that of his womenfolk was even more onerous, particularly as they were responsible both for tending to the needs of the keeper and keeping house. Grace Darling was later to write: 'I have seven apartments in the house to keep in a state fit to be inspected everyday by Gentlemen.'

No doubt this meant a level of spit and polish of military precision – you could probably have eaten off the floor! In addition, Grace learned how to handle boats – an ability that required skilled use of strength at all times.

left: Coloured engraving by Lieutenant Edward Johnson RN, showing *The Lower Light on Inner Farne*, 1817

right: The Longstone Lighthouse on the Outer Farne

On 7 September 1838, a violent storm forced the passenger steamer *SS Forfarshire* onto the rocks of Big Harcar, a mile from the lighthouse. Of the sixty people on board, nine escaped in the ship's boat, and another nine survived the night clinging to the remains of the broken hull on the rocks. At dawn, William and Grace Darling saw these desperate people and launched their own boat to the rescue.

This boat still exists in the Grace Darling National Memorial Museum at Bamburgh in Northumberland. It is a small coble, about 20 feet (6m) long and 4 feet (1.2m) wide, of a strong and heavy construction. Many have inaccurately referred to it as being flat-bottomed, but it is a fine sea boat of an ancient traditional design, built to launch and recover through surf. Rowing it in calm water would test three or four strong men today. In 1838, a twenty-two-year-old woman and her father launched it into a major storm and rowed a distance of at least two miles, taking into account the wind and tide. The action of merely launching this boat in such conditions is almost unthinkable; rowing it miles to the wreck and back is inconceivable to us today. But to them, it was an achievable, albeit dangerous, task. (In 1909, at nearby Newbiggin, seven fishermen drowned when their coble, the same size as the Darlings' boat, capsized in a storm while attempting a rescue from a wreck.)

When they reached the remains of the *Forfarshire*, William leapt onto the rocks to assess the situation. Alone in the boat, Grace rowed up and down until he was ready to take off five of the survivors. Back at the lighthouse, she and her mother comforted them with food, drink and warmth, while William returned alone to gather the remaining four from the rocks.

At first, only the local newspapers commented on this exceptional feat, but once the national papers got hold of the story, Grace became famous throughout the British Empire. Artists flocked to paint her portrait and to sculpt busts of her; the young Queen Victoria sent her a personal message; and life-saving organisations showered her with awards, including a specially minted gold medal from the Royal Humane Society. Journalists and poets flew ever further into daftness in their embroidery of her life and character. Demands for interviews, requests for locks of hair, and much more grew to a frenzy, but, in spite of privately expressing her distaste for such publicity, Grace always remained true to herself. In answer to an interviewer's question, she responded:

You requested me to let you know whether I felt pleasure to be out in a rough sea, which I can assure you there is none, I think, to any person in their sober senses … . I have had occasion to be in the boat with my Father for want of better help, but never at the saving of lives before, and I pray God I may never be again.

The bravery of Grace Darling is commemorated in the Central Hall at Wallington, near Morpeth in Northumberland. In 1856, the owners of Wallington, Sir Walter Trevelyan and his wife Pauline, commissioned the Pre-Raphaelite painter William Bell Scott to decorate the walls of the Hall with paintings of 'the history and worthies of Northumbria'. Grace Darling, whose picture was completed in 1860, appears alongside such luminaries as King Egfrid, St Cuthbert and the Venerable Bede.

By this time, Grace had been dead for eighteen years. After her heroic rescue of the passengers from the *Forfarshire*, she lived on at the Longstone for a tragically short period, dying from tuberculosis at the age of twenty-six in 1842. Through her own simplicity and strength, she remains an example even today, especially to anyone who is of the sea. You can visit the Grace Darling National Memorial Museum in Bamburgh, which is looked after by the Royal National Lifeboat Institution (museum due for refurbishment at time of going to press. For details, tel: 01668 214465).

left: William Bell Scott's painting, *Grace Darling and her father rescuing survivors from the* SS Forfarshire *in 1838*, in the Central Hall at Wallington, Northumberland

below: A traditional coble, of the type used by William and Grace Darling in 1838, with Lindisfarne Castle in the background

Souter

Souter Lighthouse is located on the north-east coast, between the Rivers Tyne and Wear. The first selection of the site was Souter Point, but in 1870 it was decided that the higher cliffs at Lizard Point were more suitable. To avoid confusion with the Lizard Lighthouse in Cornwall, Souter was retained for the name.

This stretch of coast, between South Shields and Sunderland, was proving highly dangerous for shipping. In 1869, twenty vessels came to grief, in particular on the rocks of Whitburn Steel off Whitburn and Marsden. Despite the coming of the railways, it still proved cheaper to transport coal and iron by sea, and the traffic from Newcastle and Sunderland was therefore rapidly increasing. The heavy industry of this area was also causing pollution that combined with sea fog to make conditions very hazardous.

Souter was commissioned in 1870 by Trinity House from their Chief Engineer, James Douglass. Like Robert Stevenson, he came from a dynasty of lighthouse builders. His father, Nicholas, was Superintendent Engineer to Trinity House, while his brother, William, was in charge of all the lighthouses in Ireland. He cut his teeth helping his father to construct Bishop Rock Lighthouse in the Scillies in 1847, and was responsible for the last Eddystone light *(see p.29)*, as well as lighthouses at Wolf Rock off Land's End and Smalls Rock near Milford Haven in Pembrokeshire, where he was given up for dead when his building party was engulfed by a storm in 1859.

At Souter, Douglass designed a 75-foot tower of rubble masonry covered in Portland cement. To provide shelter, the ancillary buildings were laid out landward of the lighthouse, and consisted of a square courtyard with covered corridor, accommodating the engine and boiler houses, a coke store, workshop, storeroom and six houses for staff and their families. Huge tanks were incorporated into the foundations of the inner courtyard to store rainwater to feed the boilers.

Souter was very advanced technically. It was the first lighthouse in the world to be lit by electricity, using Professor Holmes's alternating current magneto-electric generator that had been displayed at the Paris Universal Exhibition in 1867 *(see p.23)*. Although a back-up emergency system was installed using an oil lamp, the electric light failed only twice in eight years. On one occasion, smoke from testing the emergency oil lamp masked the electrical contact, and the second was the result of a keeper falling asleep on watch.

To focus the light, a rotating octagonal drum was built within the lantern. Each side of this drum consisted of seven vertical lenses that condensed and reflected the light out to sea in a series of distinct but adjoining beams. The battery of lenses multiplied the original light 230 times, giving a power equivalent to 700,000 candles (remember the 24 candles of Smeaton's first Eddystone light, *see p.21*). The effect of the light was recorded by Major Elliott, an American lighthouse expert, in 1871: 'After leaving the Tyne at night we stood off from Souter Point to observe the light from the sea, and it certainly surpassed in brilliancy any I have ever seen.'

Douglass's ingenuity extended to the Middle Light. Realising that in earlier lighthouses, half the light cast was effectively wasted as the revolving beam swept inland, he borrowed this wasted light and reflected it downwards by means of a series of prisms to mark several groups of dangerous rocks in Sunderland Bay.

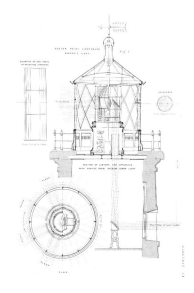

left: James Douglass; lithograph by G.B. Black, 1879

above: Douglass's design for the Souter lantern

Two black foghorns stand on top of their own building to the east of Souter Lighthouse *(see p.24)*. They are the successors of a single horn provided by Professor Holmes in 1871. The original horn was shaped like a clay pipe and faced straight out to sea. It was replaced by a pair, of similar shape, angled to project the noise up and down the coast – vital for an area particularly susceptible to sea fog. The present horns are trumpet-shaped and, although smaller than their predecessors, even more powerful.

When visibility fell below two miles in the daytime, or when the lights of the Tyne and Wear piers could not be made out at night, the horns let out a four-second blast every 45 seconds. The effect was, apparently, ear-shattering, and keepers were paid an extra two-pence an hour 'noise money' as compensation for the din. The local residents were not so fortunate, but in 1988 were put out of their misery when the foghorns ceased to blow.

When Souter Lighthouse was first built, the six houses that provided accommodation for the keepers and their families represented an isolated community, although today the village of Marsden surrounds them. The National Trust has restored one of the keepers' houses to give an idea of what life was like in the late nineteenth century.

The ancillary buildings and keepers' cottages

The working staff in the 1870s consisted of a qualified engineer in overall charge, with four assistant keepers. The latter were all in their twenties, but had already had experience at one of Trinity House's prototype electric lighthouses at Dungeness and South Foreland in Kent. This meant that few of the early keepers were local men: they came from as far afield as Milford Haven in Pembrokeshire, Portland in Dorset and Harwich, Trinity House's depot, in Essex.

By 1881, the census shows that some of the keepers had been joined by their families. The engineer's household consisted of his wife, eight children, an unmarried sister and a servant. One of the assistant lighthouse keepers was Robert Darling, nephew of the famous Grace *(see pp.40-41)*, who was to work at Souter for twenty-four years. Each of the six houses had its own stone-walled front garden and backyard with wash-house, lavatory and fuel store. A little entrance porch opened onto the central staircase hall, flanked downstairs by kitchen and parlour (that could double as the parents' bedroom), and two bedrooms upstairs. Interconnecting doors between the houses allowed for extra bedrooms for large families in the houses of unmarried keepers.

Douglass described the routine at Souter:

The watches of four hours each are kept by the four assistant keepers, one of whom is required to be constantly in the engine or boiler room, and one in the lantern, throughout the night between sunset and sunrise. Communication is established by speaking tubes between the engine room and lantern, also between the lantern and the bedroom of each lightkeeper.

The kitchen in one of the keeper's cottages, refurnished by the National Trust to indicate how it may have looked at the end of the nineteenth century

Orford Ness

Orford Ness in Suffolk is the largest shingle spit in Europe, a bleak and desolate promontory of saltmarshes, mudflats and brackish lagoons. Being flat and without any distinguishing features, it posed a constant threat to shipping on a route that was vital to London's coal trade. By the late Middle Ages, timber had become a relatively rare commodity, to be used for building ships and houses rather than burned as fuel. Instead, sea coal, so called because it was brought down from Newcastle upon Tyne and other north-eastern ports by ship, was the fuel that heated London's homes and provided the power for its industries. One legend has it that the famous Lord Mayor of London, Richard Whittington (c.1358-1423) made his fortune by trading in coals brought to London in sailing vessels called 'cats' – hence the story of Dick Whittington and his Cat.

One of the reasons why Trinity House was given its charter in the sixteenth century *(see pp.12-13)* was to provide some kind of protection for the east coast, in particular the vulnerable section around Lowestoft.

However, the lucrative income that could be derived from dues meant that many lighthouses were built by private enterprise, and Orford is a case in point. Medieval records indicate that there was some sort of lighthouse on the Ness as early as 1381. During an overnight storm in 1627, no less than 32 ships were wrecked here, and a few years later the courtier Sir John Meldrum petitioned Charles I for the right to build a series of lighthouses to protect the increasing volume of shipping transporting coal. Having also acquired the rights to North and South Foreland in Kent, Meldrum sold his interest in Orford Ness to Alderman Gerard Gore, who immediately erected two wooden towers. Placed one in front of the other, the taller structure at the rear was designed to support a coal fire on its summit, while the lower building held a lantern powered by candles. This arrangement was the first of at least 11 lighthouses on Orford Ness, many of which succeeded earlier structures swept away by the constant battering of the North Sea tides against the shifting shingle.

Orford Ness Lighthouse perched on the edge of the receding shingle bank

In 1648 Gore employed the daughter and widow of two of his former keepers, Mrs Bradshaw. Presumably she must have failed dismally in her duties as lightkeeper, for he was forced to write her a harsh letter of dismissal:

According to my promise, you have enjoyed the Light now till Xmas and I have had more complaints in this half year than ever I had in your father or your husband's time. I did not think you would have been so careless but I excuse you because you are a woman.

Unfortunately, this situation was only the first of a series of problems over the next 70 years. The lights at Orford continued to be supervised by private, wealthy individuals who did not regard them as a priority. In spite of frequent complaints to Trinity House – prompting one of the keepers to counter that 'the east wind doth darken the light' – matters deteriorated so much that passing ships were refusing to pay any dues. As if to compound the problems, a naval press gang took a keeper in 1690 and on 23 June 1702, the lighthouses were attacked by French pirates, who broke the lantern and made off with several items, including the keepers' beds. Meanwhile, the sea was also taking its toll. Having washed away the lower of the two towers in 1691, it promptly and efficiently removed its replacement in 1710. Two brick towers superseded the wooden lighthouses, but again the lower front light was swept away by the sea. Two later timber lights burned down, probably as a result of incompetence on the part of the keepers, and yet another lower tower was swept away.

This unsatisfactory state of affairs was resolved at the end of the eighteenth century, when a stone lighthouse, built by local architect William Wilkins, was sited further inland from the perilous position on the headland occupied by its predecessors, and therefore had a fighting chance of survival. It was acquired by Trinity House in 1836 in the great sweep-up of lighthouses *(see p.14)*. Fifty years later, red and green shades were installed to form guiding sectors, and a revolving lens was introduced in 1914 to produce a white flash every five seconds. With the provision of electrical power and back-up generators in 1959, the keepers were finally relieved and their accommodation was demolished.

A keeper at Orford Ness mounting a black cone as a storm warning for local shipping

Further innovations took place in 1964, when the old stone lighthouse became the first in the country to be remotely controlled from Harwich. Today, Trinity House continues to own and administer Orford Ness Lighthouse, and it has become the most powerful light on the east coast of England. The Ness itself, a secret military test site from 1913 until the mid-1980s, was acquired by the National Trust in 1993, and is now an internationally important nature reserve.

George Carter, who was born in Aldeburgh and served on Trinity House lightships during the Second World War, remembered when he was a young boy:

A small cottage, always within hearing of the sea … . Up the narrow dark stairs lay my bedroom, with its iron bedstead with huge brass knobs … . I liked the other bedroom best, for at night one could see the light of Orfordness Lighthouse, and the huge white shaft of its beam swept in through the window and illuminated every crack and cranny.

Inspired by this reassuring beam, Carter resolved to find out how the light worked, and trudged 12 miles across the shingle one autumn afternoon, fortified only with a packet of sandwiches:

At last I reached the red and white tower of the lighthouse. I saw one of the keepers, and asked him if I might see the lantern as I had tramped many miles to do so. But he refused, and despite my persuasion, remained obdurate. Disconsolately I began my weary homeward tramp, dusk was falling and I was filled with a vague uneasy feeling at the thought of being alone in that vast and grim desolation at night … . It was eerie, walking on shingle in the dark. My footsteps started small avalanches, which rattled behind me in the most uncanny way. … At last, when the friendly twinkling lights of the town were close at hand, I took to my heels and ran as if the Devil himself were at my heels.

Carter's account of Orford Ness, still a beautiful but wild and desolate landscape, gives some idea of the isolation endured by the keepers of the lights on this exposed and ever-shifting coastline. And, as with so many of its predecessors, it seems the Orford Ness Lighthouse that has stood on that fragile shore since 1792 will itself succumb to the waves within the next ten years.

below: Orford Ness Lighthouse at dawn

right: The mainland village of Orford from the Ness. A thriving port in the early Middle Ages, it lost the lucrative east coast trade with the growth of the Ness

South Foreland

The chalk cliffs of Dover represent one of the symbolic landscapes of Britain. Here the North Downs run into the English Channel, with cliffs formed from the fossil remains of a myriad of microscopic sea creatures. In the sunlight the cliffs are a brilliant white, and sharp-eyed Romans looking out from the shores of Gaul may have called the mysterious island Albion from *alba*, the Latin for white, as a result. When shrouded in misty rain, they can look a wan grey, while sunrise and sunset imbue them with a golden glow.

South Foreland Lighthouse stands on Langdon Cliffs, and for centuries has guided mariners through the notoriously dangerous shoals and banks of the Goodwin Sands, which were known as 'the Great Ship Swallower'. The present lighthouse was developed in 1843 upon the site of two earlier lights, one of which was built in 1643. It has a Victorian touch of romance. One almost expects to see Rapunzel's golden hair flowing down from this Gothic castle tower with all its trimmings. That aside, as at Souter *(see pp.42-45)*, it was built as much for comfort as its comparatively remote location permitted, but it is more compact.

South Foreland Lighthouse at dusk, with its adjoining keepers' cottages

The keeper and his chief assistant lived in two fully interconnecting houses attached to the lighthouse.

South Foreland is not one light, but two, both now redundant. Away on the eastern cliff-edge stands a little companion, a clearing light – one which says to mariners, 'keep to this side of me if you want to miss the obstruction I guard'. Between these lights stood the great boiler house and generators with houses and works that made this place significant. All of these vanished under a mansion built in the 1920s for members of the Cunard family. They continued the eccentricity of the castle tower by using the old clearing light as a summerhouse, and building the little windmill generator next to it to provide power for their home.

The keepers and their families had to be fairly self-sufficient, and the large area of gardens can be traced, with various plots dedicated to particular crops. At the western corner are the remarkably intact stables that were used for horses to provide transport to Dover and Ramsgate. What cannot be seen now are the piggeries, which were very much a feature of land-based lighthouse communities – pigs eat waste and return a whole host of useable products, including muck to fertilise the land. These, together with the lavatories and boiler houses to cook up food for the pigs and chickens, are now under the Cunard house.

A painting of South Foreland Lighthouse by Lesley Hepherd, entitled *Walking the Dog, c.* 1950

South Foreland played an important part in the development of electricity for lighthouses. Originally the light was lit by oil. But during the late 1840s and early 1850s, Trinity House conducted the first truly successful experiments, first with direct current limelight and then with an alternating current. This was cutting-edge technology for the time – we must bear in mind that Michael

Faraday had only discovered the possibility of an electric motor in 1821 *(see p.22).*

South Foreland may have led the way with the first electrically-powered light in the British Isles, but once out of sight of land, ships were still entirely isolated. The need to communicate not only with ships but also lightships and off-shore establishments grew as the nineteenth century proceeded. For this, the telegraph and other known methods broke down because they depended on vulnerable cable links. Waiting in the wings was another world first: Guglielmo Marconi and his invention of wireless telegraphy.

On Christmas Eve 1898, Marconi set up an experimental link between South Foreland and the East Goodwin lightship, over a distance of 12 miles. The weather was characteristically foul, causing Marconi's devoted assistant, George Kemp, to suffer a prolonged bout of seasickness aboard the lightship. The first message he sent was Christmas greetings to relations

ashore and to the editors of all the major newspapers.

Less than three months later, on 11 March 1899, the link proved invaluable. A full-rigged ship, the *Elbe* of Hamburg, inward bound with a cargo of slates from Nantes, went aground in darkness and thick fog on the Goodwin Sands. The South Goodwin lightship fired rocket signals that were heard by the newly-equipped East Goodwin. Mr East, the Marconi operator, wirelessed George Kemp at South Foreland with the news. From there, Kemp performed the world's first alert of a lifeboat by wireless message when he telephoned Ramsgate, who launched a tug to aid the stranded ship, with the lifeboat from Kingsdown following. The *Elbe* refloated 8 hours later with their joint assistance.

In the same year, the lighthouse was part of yet another first, when wireless messages were exchanged across the Channel between South Foreland and Wimereux near Boulogne in France.

Beachy Head

The towering white cliffs of Beachy Head and the Seven Sisters on the East Sussex coast have in themselves long been a landmark for mariners in the English Channel. The earliest records of a light being mounted on Beachy Head date from the late seventeenth century, when it is believed that local people lit a fire beacon to warn ships at sea of foreign privateers lurking in wait beyond the headland. This early warning system of peril at sea was taken more seriously during the Napoleonic Wars, when an official naval station was established on the cliffs.

Although a request for a lighthouse was passed to Trinity House in 1691, it was not until 1828 that the first building was constructed 280 feet above sea level, on the cliff-top just west of Beachy Head. This relatively short lighthouse, just 49 feet in height and known as Belle Tout, was equipped with Argand lamps on a revolving platform, which provided a clear and prolonged flash every two minutes.

Beachy Head Lighthouse

However, as with many other lighthouses built on the top of cliffs, it was frequently obscured by cloud and fog, and was finally abandoned in 1899.

Although restored and occupied as a private house in the 1930s, Belle Tout was used by British and Canadian artillery for target practice during the Second World War. Amazingly, it survived this onslaught, and was later restored by the BBC in 1988, who used it as a film set in Fay Weldon's *Life and Loves of a She Devil*. In January 1999, Belle Tout's perilous position on the South Downs was highlighted when a vast swathe of chalk cliff crashed into the sea. With only 10 feet left between the building and oblivion, its then owners embarked on a successful project to move it, on steel rails, to a safer site 50 feet back, thus ensuring the building's survival for perhaps another hundred years.

Having abandoned Belle Tout in 1899, Trinity House built the existing tower lighthouse at the base of the cliffs. This massive structure, designed by Sir Thomas Matthews and built in huge blocks of Cornish granite, was erected in record time by mounting a steel dam around the site and pumping out the water, thereby allowing the builders to work almost continuously, regardless of tides or weather. Rising to nearly 125 feet in height, with seven floors, the new Beachy Head Lighthouse was complete by 1902 and the paraffin vapour lamp first illuminated on 2 October.

During the Second World War, Beachy Head Lighthouse, like other coastal lights, was rarely lit. However, the keepers occasionally received official requests to fire up the lamp in order to assist British aircraft struggling home from raids over Europe. As the original paraffin vapour lamp took at least fifteen minutes to light, the keepers came up with the ingenious solution of dashing upstairs with their kitchen lamp. Former Principal Keeper Reginald Simon recalled that: 'The rays were much narrower but the light served its purpose. It was only required for short periods – sometimes five minutes – when word would come via the signal station – "OK, they have gone over".'

On one occasion during the war, the lighthouse and its keepers narrowly avoided obliteration, as Mr Simon remembered:

… a mine was observed drifting towards the station, we passed the word to the naval authorities and were told that if it was over 200 yards away to attempt to sink it by gun fire. We told whoever it was at the other end that we had no guns, and after a slight hesitation he said, "Well, just standby". It continued to drift towards us and in a few minutes it passed with no more than three feet to spare, heading for the shore where it struck a rock and exploded, blackening the cliff to the very top.

In 1975, Beachy Head Lighthouse was provided with mains electricity, allowing the keepers finally to abandon the smelly paraffin equipment they had used for nearly seventy years. Less than ten years later, in 1983, the lighthouse went automatic and the three keepers came ashore for the last time.

The Needles

For hundreds of years, ships attempting to reach either Southampton or Portsmouth from the western approach have faced the perils of negotiating their way through a narrow channel into the safety of the Solent. On the right (or starboard) side, at the western extremity of the Isle of Wight, are the sharp, precipitous chalk stacks known as the Needles. On the left (or port) side, vessels are hemmed in by the shifting sand spits of the Shingles Bank, which protrude from the mainland and culminate at Hurst Point. In the days of sailing ships, and with the added disadvantage of strong tides, this passage could only be taken in daylight and under good weather conditions.

In 1781, a group of local shipmasters and merchants asked Trinity House to provide lighthouses in order to alleviate this problem, arguing cogently that 'ships and vessels have been lost … and the lives, ships and goods of His Majesty's subjects as well as the King's Royal Navy continue to be exposed to the like calamities more especially in the night time and in hard southerly gales'. After several years of delay, and an unsuccessful attempt to lease the construction of the new lighthouses to one of the petitioning merchants, Trinity House finally took responsibility for the project in November 1785. Just nine months later, in the autumn of 1786, three new lighthouses had been completed: one alongside Henry VIII's Hurst Castle; a second high on St Catherine's Down on the southern headland of the Isle of Wight *(see p.67)*; and a third on top of the cliffs above the Needles.

Although the mainland lighthouse at Hurst Point served satisfactorily until 1860, the cliff-top towers at St Catherine's and the Needles were quickly abandoned. All too often, and particularly when strong south-westerly airstreams were prominent, both lighthouses became obliterated by thick clouds and fog, ironically at the time when clear guiding lights for shipping were most crucial.

The Needles at sunset

above: The view of the Needles from the Old Battery

right: A mural in the Old Battery by Geoff Campion showing a First World War soldier

Much to the dismay of the local merchants, it was to be another 70 years before the problem of the Needles light was tackled again. Finally, in 1858, the Trinity House architect, James Walker, built the new Needles Lighthouse, at a cost of £20,000, on the chalk stack or 'needle' furthest from the land, where it remains to this day. The construction work involved excavating deep into the rock on which the lighthouse stands in order to sink substantial foundations, but this also created a cavity in which to house fresh-water tanks below the tower. Once the Needles Lighthouse had been illuminated for the first time on 1 January 1859, it became something of an attraction for visitors, including the newly-married Prince and Princess of Wales (later King Edward VII and Queen Alexandra), who toured it in 1863.

The relatively easy access to the Needles Lighthouse meant that, while keepers elsewhere came to be relieved by helicopter, the men on this isolated chalk stack continued to be transported, and supplied, by boat from Yarmouth. This continued until 1987, when a helipad was installed on top of Walker's lantern. However, occasionally the keepers on the Needles were among the first to benefit from improvements to their monotonous way of life. Mike Williams, a Trinity House Principal Keeper, recalled that they were the second lighthouse (Bishop Rock being the first) to receive a television set, in the early 1960s:

The one on the Needles was donated by the Lymington Flower Club, and it had an inscription on it saying [so].

Not only did they present the television but they also repaired it because it used to break down quite often. I don't know why TV wasn't supplied [sooner]; perhaps because a keeper might watch it when he was on duty.

The keepers at the Needles finally left their posts on 8 December 1994, since when the lighthouse has been controlled automatically from Harwich. Today, visitors to the Needles Old Battery, a nineteenth-century fort on the headland, can inspect some of the original foghorns removed from the lighthouse when it was automated in 1994. The National Trust, which acquired the Old Battery in 1975, also plays host to the submarine cable providing electric power for the lighthouse, which runs across the site and never fails to fascinate visiting schoolchildren.

BUT THE ENEMY NEVER CAME....

St Catherine's Point

The lighthouse perched right on top of St Catherine's Down, on the southernmost tip of the Isle of Wight, is in some ways an enigma. In this magical place, overlooking the English Channel, it is known as the Oratory and nicknamed the Pepper Pot. Standing 35 feet tall, with its octagonal shape and four opposed buttresses, in mist or low light the tower could be mistaken for a lost rocket, set up and pointing to the stars. Indeed, many of Britain's attempts at military rockets *were* tested on High Down not far away, towards the Needles.

It is, in fact, an ancient fire-basket light, and legend has it that it was set up in penance for wrong-doing in about 1328. Fifteen years earlier, the *Ste Marie de Bayonne*, loaded down with 174 casks of wine from Tonnay in Aquitaine, had been wrecked at Chale at the foot of St Catherine's Down. The wine was allegedly bound for the monastery of Livers in Picardy in northern France, and was owned by three men of Gascony, which meant that it came under the governance of the King of England,

Edward II. The local lord of the manor, Walter de Godyton, gathered together some friends and 'took over' or bought 53 of the casks recovered by the locals from the wreck. He seems to have had the right to do so, but the law arriving on the island decided otherwise, charged him with illegally receiving goods and fined him heavily. Since the wine was destined for a monastery, he was furthermore threatened by the Pope with excommunication and eternal damnation. To prevent this, he offered to build the tower and light on St Catherine's Down, with an oratory and priest to pray for the souls of mariners.

While the shipwreck of the *Ste Marie de Bayonne* is on record, recent research suggests that the tower is older than this story, so maybe Walter only converted it to a light. His family cared for it for 200 years, until the Oratory was closed under Henry VIII's Dissolution of the Monasteries. The octagonal structure does not seem to have been used for a light since then, but survives remarkably intact.

St Catherine's Oratory (The Pepper Pot)

Nearby is the tower of the lighthouse commissioned in 1786 from Richard Jupp, a Surveyor to the East India Company, which fell out of commission in the mid-nineteenth century, because its head was all too often above the clouds. This conical structure is, naturally, now referred to as the Salt Cellar.

In 1836, Trinity House finally addressed the problem of what to do with St Catherine's Point, and commissioned James Walker to build a crenellated octagonal tower rising in a series of diminishing tiers. However, this lighthouse was found to be too tall and the top two tiers were removed in 1875. Although fog could still obliterate the top on occasion, it has survived and remains in service. In 1932, a smaller copy of the main lighthouse was built in front of it to accommodate new fog-signal apparatus. Inevitably a nickname followed, and the two towers are known as the 'Cow and Calf'.

St Catherine's Lighthouse

The Lizard

The Lizard Peninsula in Cornwall is the most southerly point of mainland Britain. Here the National Trust owns farmland and cliffs that surround a lighthouse of great interest, with two towers, although only one now has a light on it.

The first lighthouse was built on Lizard Point in 1619, and there is no need to ask why. A glance seaward at most states of the tide shows broken water; when this has receded, a jagged array of rocks is revealed.

The lighthouse was sponsored privately by Sir John Killigrew of Arwenack, Falmouth, but faced stiff opposition from local inhabitants, who protested that they would 'receive no more benefit by shipwreck, for this will prevent it'. Having spent £500 building the lighthouse, Killigrew hoped to recoup his money with voluntary contributions from passing ships, but these failed to materialise and with the added maintenance costs,

including ten shillings' worth of fuel every night, he was forced to petition James I for the right to charge compulsory dues. The patent, granted in 1623 and enabling him to charge ship-owners half a penny per ton of cargo when passing Lizard Point, caused such an outcry that the tax was withdrawn, the light was extinguished, and Killigrew's tower gradually fell into ruins.

Mariners had to wait until 1752, when the owner of Lizard Point,

Thomas Fonnereau, with the support of Trinity House, completed a new lighthouse with twin towers and a cottage in between. The two lights on two towers made the Lizard instantly recognisable and distinguishable from the single light at St Agnes in the Scilly Isles and the three lights on the Casquets in the Channel Islands. Most importantly, the relationship between the two lights, as seen from the sea, provided a series of views, or transits, to warn mariners of the huge width of the reef.

At first, these lights were powered by coal fires in brick hearths, surrounded by windows made up of small panes of leaded glass mounted in wooden frames. Highly-paid men were employed to hump coal up the stairs, and then keep the fires bright by blowing them with bellows. A keeper was delegated to recline on a couch in the cottage below, from where he could view both lanterns through the windows. If his colleagues flagged and the fires dimmed, he would remind them of their duties with a blast on a cow horn, perhaps the only example of Trinity House paying an employee to lie down on the job!

The Lizard Lighthouse flashing its light at dusk

Trinity House assumed full responsibility for the lights in 1771, and replaced the smoky, expensive and troublesome fires in 1812 with Argand lamps. In 1821, structural improvements were made, including the construction of houses for the keepers, leaving the station looking very much as it does today. The Lizard Lighthouses were among the first to be powered by electricity, in 1878, but it was not until 1903 that a revolving light was installed in the eastern tower. The western light was closed down, and its tower was later converted into a fog-signal house. With this added facility, the station required a minimum of eight keepers, all of whom lived on site with their wives and, at one point,

up to forty-five children. The light was finally automated in 1998 and remains the functioning lighthouse today.

The Lizard Lighthouse is still owned by Trinity House, but its buildings are maintained and opened to the public by the Trevithick Trust. An old hotel beneath its walls was recently restored by the National Trust to create a five-star youth hostel. Of further interest nearby is the old castellated Lloyds Signal House (now a private house), which was used to send signals to ships coming up the Channel and to transmit news of their voyages direct to Lloyds in London. Guglielmo Marconi has connections here, as at South Foreland *(see pp.58-59)*.

Marconi's Lizard Station was set up at Bass Point in order to conduct experiments towards his ultimate aim of transmitting messages by wireless across the Atlantic. In January 1901, the first signals from Niton on the Isle of Wight were received by Marconi at the Lizard Station, over a distance of 186 miles. Less than a year later, on 12 December, Marconi received the first transatlantic message at Signal Hill, Newfoundland, where he and his assistant Kemp clearly heard the three dots of the letter 'S', sent in Morse code from Poldhu in Cornwall. Marconi's small timber-framed station at Bass Point on the Lizard Peninsula has been restored by the National Trust, and was opened to the public in 2001.

The lifeboat station on the Lizard. By the time the station was closed in 1961, the lifeboat had been launched 136 times and saved 562 lives

The Gribbin

The Gribbin in Cornwall is not in fact a lighthouse, but a daymark, which caters for a hazard that was present at the dawn of seafaring and remains with us – getting lost in broad daylight.

One of the first things that navigators like Captain Cook did when surveying a newly discovered coastline was to sail along it on a safe offing, or send companions out in small boats to paint and draw profiles of the land set before them.

As they did this, they named features – headlands, inlets, inland mountains, and other features visible to them. Many of these pictures, when viewed hundreds of years later, are still remarkably accurate. However, even when armed with the comfort of a chart, it is possible to go horribly wrong. So daymarks, such as crosses, cairns or mounds, were built so that sailors could pass to each other precise descriptions of the hazards to be avoided.

Gribbin Head lies west of Fowey. In spite of centuries of experience, some mariners heading for Falmouth, further west along the Cornish coast, approached the Gribbin in the mistaken assumption that it was St Anthony Head and the route into the deep waters of the Carrick Roads and Falmouth Harbour. Instead, they found themselves ensnared by the perilous shallows of St Austell Bay. The early use of local landmarks, including a windmill and two chapels

on the headlands either side of Fowey Harbour, proved unsatisfactory, and in 1832 Trinity House built the daymark.

It stands on land donated by William Rashleigh of Menabilly, who also provided the building stone from his quarry nearby and a quay for landing materials on his beach at Polridmouth, just to the east. Such generosity came only with the desire that Trinity House should 'make the Beacon an ornament to my grounds'. They most properly rose to the

challenge, issuing a specification for tender for the erection of a 'very handsome Greco Gothic Square Tower'. The result, standing 84-feet high, resembles a Doric column made square, topped by a Gothic castle.

One corner points to sea and, from its earliest days, the two faces thus exposed to the mariner have been painted red and white, barber-pole style. Now restored by the National Trust, resplendent in its paint and with its base railing

replaced, it stands as a destination and challenge to walkers on the Cornish Coastal Path, who may climb to the top on summer Sundays for the reward of unmatched views. Most importantly, it still fulfils the function for which it was built, a well-loved warning to all who ply the seas of this coast.

The Gribbin Head with its candy-striped daymark

Lundy

Lundy is an island lying smack bang in the middle of the entrance to the Bristol Channel, once one of the busiest waterways in the world, and still host to some very heavy shipping. It is both an anchorage of shelter and a huge hazard, especially in the vast tides hereabouts and bad visibility. Wrecks have been common.

Beacons were established on Lundy, but there was no lighthouse until 1819 when Bristol merchants offered finance. Trinity House surveyed Beacon Hill, the highest point on the island, as the site for a new light. The impressive granite installation was completed in 1820: its uncompromising solidity coupled with Georgian taste was the work of Daniel Alexander, not only the architect of the lighthouses at Harwich and the Inner Farne *(see p.38)*, but also Dartmoor Prison and Maidstone Gaol.

Old Light looks so permanent and purposeful, so what could have gone wrong and why are there now two other lights built down near the sea, to the north and south? Setting a tower as high as possible on a hill makes it visible over a far range, but nobody took into consideration the fact that the hill was often shrouded in mist in bad weather. By 1891 the light was replaced by the North and South Lights, but Old Light was so massive that it just stayed where it was. Today the fine keepers' accommodation, still connected with the tower, provides holiday accommodation organised by the Landmark Trust *(see p.90)*.

The Old Light on Lundy, close to the memorial stones of an early Christian cemetery

Despite the new lights, a remarkable wreck occurred in 1907. *HMS Montagu*, a large Duncan Class battleship only five years into her service and therefore to all intents and purposes brand new, met her doom spectacularly on Shutter Point. The Royal Navy, keen to get into the new discipline of wireless, was conducting tests and chose *HMS Montagu* to go into the Bristol Channel to steam up and down between Lundy and the receiving station at Land's End. On 25 May 1907 she came to anchor off Lundy and that evening, being apparently set for fine weather, cruised off at about 8.00pm. By midnight she was in fog, and a decision was made to return to Lundy, about 2 miles off the southern side. The captain and navigating officer thought that they were making for Hartland Point on the North Devon coast when they actually hit Lundy at 2.00am – the shock must have been considerable.

Both were disciplined in the following court martial, and rightly so, but the combination of fog and concentration on the radio experiment seems to have caused them disorientation.

The wreck soon proved a tourist attraction; the recovery of her armament and other equipment was closely followed and souvenirs taken. The remains are still a popular site for divers.

View past a granite stack to Lundy South Lighthouse, with the Devon coast on the horizon

Rathlin Island

Rathlin Island, just five and a half miles long and with a maximum breadth of one and a quarter miles, is situated off the North Antrim coast of Northern Ireland. With its steep and precipitous cliffs, rising to nearly 450 feet above sea level on the north and west sides of the island, it has long provided a vantage point for the observation of local shipping. In the early years of the eighteenth century, a French privateer took up permanent residence in order to survey his potential victims from the heights, while two and a half centuries later, the coastguards stationed on the cliffs monitored the passage of the life-saving convoys sailing from the United States to Britain during the Second World War.

In January 1758, the Rev. John Gage, who had purchased Rathlin Island two years earlier, presented a petition to the Irish Parliament in which he 'humbly proposed a scheme to Parliament to render the collieries on the northern coast of Ireland more useful, the navigation in and out of St George's Channel more safe and other purposes for the advantage and safety of the Channel trade'.

Rathlin East Lighthouse on the cliffs above Alta Cory Bay

In addition to suggesting the construction of harbours on Rathlin, to provide shelter for large ships that could then be loaded with coal by tenders sailing from Ballycastle on the mainland, Gage advocated the building of a lighthouse on the island. However, his proposals seem to have fallen on deaf ears, and almost a century elapsed before any further progress was made, although coastguards were first employed in 1821 and housed in a row of cottages in Church Bay, alongside the landing stage.

In 1849, the Ballast Board (later the Commissioners of Irish Lights) purchased a small plot of land on the north-eastern tip of the island, where Rathlin's East Light was erected between 1849 and 1856, to the designs of George Halpin, who worked on a number of Irish lights. The first stone of the lighthouse was laid by the Rev. Robert Gage, the then owner of the island and the great-grandson of John Gage. Described by a contemporary as 'lord of the isle', Robert Gage took an active part in island affairs,

banishing his subjects 'to the continent of Ireland for misconduct, or repeated offences against the laws'. Those who committed minor offences had a cow or horse confiscated for a few days, or – in criminal cases – were forced to ingest 'a copious draught of salt water from the surrounding ocean'.

From the start, it was important to differentiate Rathlin's East Light from the lighthouse on the Scottish Mull of Kintyre, and it was therefore conceived as a fixed multi-light, in that it had a small iron-canopied lantern house to the left of the main tower. This lower light was discontinued in 1912, when a revolving apparatus was installed in the taller structure. Rathlin's West Light on Bull Point, equipped with a foghorn, was constructed in the early years of the twentieth century, and during the First World War a minor light was placed on the southernmost tip of the island at Rue Point. All three lights are still operational, and are run automatically by the Commissioners of Irish Lights - the equivalent to Trinity House.

Although the lighthouses on Rathlin Island are not isolated towers at sea, they could still be perilous places to work in times of danger. Early in the twentieth century, the captain of the White Star Canadian liner *Megantic* noticed a distress signal flying from the East Light on Alta Cory Head. Interpreting this as a request for medical assistance, he dispatched his doctor ashore in a small boat. On landing, the doctor found one of the lighthouse keepers severely injured. While cleaning the fog-gun, an unexploded charge inadvertently left in the weapon had gone off, tearing away the man's arm and causing serious burns. Fortunately, the doctor was able to dress his wounds, take him back to the ship, and deliver him safely to hospital in Liverpool. Had the liner not appeared at that moment, he would certainly have died before a doctor could have been summoned by boat from Ballycastle, nine miles away on the Irish mainland.

Rathlin Island played an important role in the development of wireless telegraphy, an invention that was to revolutionise navigation and ship-to-shore communications. In May 1898, the brilliant young Italian-Irish physicist, Guglielmo Marconi, set up his apparatus at Ballycastle and Rathlin Island, with sponsorship from Lloyds of London and the Belfast-born Lord Kelvin (who was convinced of the commercial value of wireless telegraphy). With assistance from John Cecil, a Rathlin farmer who helped to erect the poles and other equipment there, he succeeded in transmitting from the East Lighthouse to the White Lodge in Ballycastle Harbour.

Only seven months later, Marconi succeeded in sending a Christmas message from the East Goodwin lightship to South Foreland Lighthouse in Kent *(see pp.58-59)*, and in December 1901 transmitted the first signal – the letter 'S' in Morse (three dots) – from Poldhu in Cornwall across the Atlantic to Signal Hill at St John's in Newfoundland.

Guglielmo Marconi in the receiving room at Signal Hill, St John's, Newfoundland in 1901

The Lighthouse in Literature

Pharos loquitor
Far in the bosom of the deep
O'er these wild shelves my watch I keep,
A ruddy gem of changeful light
Bound on the dusky brow of night.
The seaman bids my lustre hail
And scorns to strike his tim'rous sail.

The Scottish novelist and poet Walter Scott wrote these lines in the visitors' book of the Bell Rock Lighthouse in 1810, when he accompanied Robert Stevenson on his tour of inspection. But perhaps the most famous lighthouse in English literature appears in Virginia Woolf's novel, *To the Lighthouse*, which was published in 1927.

Although Woolf located her lighthouse on the island of Skye, it was based on Godrevy Lighthouse in St Ives Bay, on the north Cornish coast. When she started to plan the writing, she intended to provide a portrait of her father, Sir Leslie Stephen, as the central character. However, it is her mother Julia who is brought to life as Mrs Ramsay, the mother who holds her large family together with an extraordinary power. Perhaps because she wished to avoid any suggestion of irreverence towards her parents, Woolf trans-ferred the setting from Cornwall to Scotland. She also wished to create an association with Sir Walter Scott, a favourite author of both

Leslie Stephen and the fictional Mr Ramsay.

Leslie Stephen fell in love with this stretch of coastline during one of his walking holidays in Cornwall in 1882, just after Virginia's birth. Enquiring about places to rent, he was recommended Talland House, an early Victorian building with views across the bay to Godrevy Lighthouse. Although the house was not furnished, Leslie Stephen spent a night there and was convinced that it would make an ideal place for his young family to take their holidays. For the next 13 years, Virginia and her sister and brothers did just that, indulging in bathing, walking and reading. The idyll came to an end with the death of her mother in 1895.

Throughout the novel, the idea of going to the Lighthouse is constantly mooted. It is also the constant presence, day and night. In one scene, Mrs Ramsay sits alone:

Losing personality, one lost the fret, the hurry, the stir; and there rose to her lips always some exclamation of triumph over life when things came together in this peace, this rest, this eternity; and pausing there she looked out to meet that stroke of the Lighthouse, the long steady stroke, the last of three, which was her stroke, for watching them in this mood always at this hour, one could

not help attaching oneself to one thing especially of the things one saw; and this thing, the long steady stroke, was her stroke.

Godrevy Lighthouse stands on Godrevy Island, which is privately owned. The National Trust owns Godrevy Point on the mainland, and a coastal walk that provides views of the lighthouse has been devised by Christina Hardyment in *Literary Trails: Writers in their Landscapes*, which was published by the National Trust in 2000.

left: Godrevy Lighthouse at sunset

below: The painted fireplace in Virginia Woolf's bedroom at Monk's House in East Sussex, decorated with an image of Godrevy Lighthouse

The Lighthouse in Art

Lighthouses have frequently been depicted by artists over the centuries. Often the early owners and builders commissioned paintings as a commemorative mark of their achievements, as was the case in 1708, when Colonel John Lovett paid the marine artist, Isaac Sailmaker, to paint four pictures of his new Eddystone Lighthouse, built to replace Winstanley's structure, which was destroyed in the Great Storm of 1703 *(see p.26)*. One of these four paintings was presented by Lovett to his father-in-law, Sir John Verney, 1st Viscount Fermanagh, and it can still be seen at his home, Claydon House in Buckinghamshire, now owned by the National Trust.

Artistic interest in lighthouses continued well into the twentieth century. In 1927, following the successful sale of a painting for $1,500, the American artist Edward Hopper splashed out on his first car,

a second-hand Dodge. With the freedom to travel to remote areas of countryside, Hopper and his wife Jo spent their summer holiday that year at Cape Elizabeth, Maine, where he produced his famous painting entitled *Lighthouse Hill*. It shows the eastern of two lighthouses on this site, both of which were built in 1874 to help mark the entrance to Portland Harbour. By 1927, the western light had been extinguished and the eastern light electrified with a beam equivalent to the power of 500,000 candles.

Edward Hopper's interest in nautical subjects first developed during his childhood on the banks of the Hudson River. Possibly his first drawing of a lighthouse was undertaken in about 1900, when he was a student at the New York School of Art. In 1916, he was inspired by the light on Monaghan Island off the Maine coast and Cape

Ann lighthouse in Massachusetts. Later in life, Hopper's love of solitude and his particular interest in painting the effects of sunlight on architecture, made the seaside location at Cape Elizabeth the ideal spot in which to indulge himself. Many of his drawings, prints and watercolours featured lighthouses, often depicted from a vantage point below the building, thus emphasising their towering aspect. During the summer of 1927 at Cape Elizabeth, he also painted the two cottages of the lighthouse keepers, Captains Berry and Upton, the latter of whom still maintained the east light. In 1929, he returned to Cape Elizabeth to paint *Lighthouse at Two Lights*, one of several pictures of this building depicted from different angles. They are a testament to his emphasis on melancholy solitude, so evident in both his urban scenes and his landscapes.

Lighthouse Hill, 1927
Edward Hopper
Oil on canvas, 29 1/16 x 40 1/4 in.
(72.82 x 102.24 cm.)
Dallas Museum of Art, gift of
Mr and Mrs Maurice Purnell, 1958.9

Lighthouse Products

The image of the lighthouse has long caught the imagination and has been reproduced as a vast range of manufactured goods. The centenary of John Smeaton's Eddystone Lighthouse off Plymouth, where a lighthouse in various forms has stood since 1698, was deemed so significant that the Royal Mint commissioned its image to appear on new coinage issued in 1860. A later image of the lighthouse was used on the penny from 1937 until its decimalisation in 1971.

Lighthouses have also been a popular theme for souvenir collectors since seaside day-trips surged in popularity during the nineteenth century. Holidaymakers could carry home tokens like thimbles, biscuit tins and the china models produced in vast quantities by the Staffordshire potters, Goss China. For years, visitors to Alum Bay on the Isle of Wight copied their Victorian forebears by taking away a glass model of a lighthouse, filled with the coloured sand for which the bay is famous.

The lighthouse is celebrated by the British Year of the Sea in 2005, with a range of products available from National Trust shops. Several Trust properties, including South Foreland Lighthouse, the White Cliffs of Dover and Souter Lighthouse, sell gift items that include bookmarks, cross-stitch kits

and photograph frames. And further afield, lighthouse collectibles are available from lighthouses, museums and specialist websites, both in the UK and abroad.

left: Lighthouse Brand salmon label, *c.*1910-20

above: Searchlight Matches, *c.*1920

right: Lighthouse tin for Lyons Assorted Toffees, incorporating a calendar, *c.*1920

National Trust Enterprises
Orderline tel: 0870 112 5384
Web: www.nationaltrust-shop.co.uk

South Foreland Lighthouse
St Margaret's Bay, Dover,
Kent CT15 6HP
Tel: 01304 852463
Email: southforeland@nationaltrust.org.uk

The White Cliffs of Dover
Gateway Visitor Centre,
Langdon Cliffs, Dover, Kent CT16 1HJ
Tel: 01304 202756
Email: whitecliffs@nationaltrust.org.uk

Souter Lighthouse
Coast Road, Whitburn, Sunderland,
Tyne and Wear SR6 7NH
Tel: 0191 529 3161
Email: souter@nationaltrust.org.uk

For museums and lighthouses,
both abroad and in the UK, see
*Lighthouse Accommodation: Britain
and Worldwide* by Joy Adcock (2003).
ISBN 0 9535182 1 3

For lighthouse-themed music, visit
www.beachcombermusic.com

See also www.nauticalia.com for a
wide range of marine and lighthouse
products.

*The information above is accurate at
the time of going to press.*

Staying in a Lighthouse

Dozens of lighthouses and their surrounding properties are available to rent for holidays, allowing visitors to get a taste of what life was like for lighthouse keepers. The National Trust owns several holiday properties attached to or close to lighthouses, including:

The Keeper's and Engineer's Cottages at Souter on the Northumberland coast, the first lighthouse in the world to be lit by electricity and one-time home of Grace Darling's nephew Robert.

Lynmouth Lighthouse Keepers' Cottage at Foreland Point on the north Devon coast, built in 1900 on the cliffs overlooking the Bristol Channel.

The Coastguard Cottages, situated above the nineteenth-century Needles Old Battery on the Isle of Wight, where visitors can see foghorns from the original lighthouse and the submarine cable which powers today's automatic lighthouse.

The Coastguard Cottages at Peppercombe, near Clovelly in north Devon. These cottages can be rented from the National Trust for holidays

For details of these and other properties, contact:
The National Trust Holiday Booking Office,
PO Box 536, Melksham,
Wiltshire SN12 8SX
Tel: 0870 4584422
Fax: 0870 4584400
Email: cottages@nationaltrust.org.uk
or visit our website:
www.nationaltrustcottages.co.uk

Trinity House Lighthouse Service, in association with Rural Retreats, also rents out lighthouse keepers' cottages on sites in England, Wales and the Channel Islands. For information, contact:
Rural Retreats,
Draycott Business Centre,
Draycott, Moreton-in-Marsh,
Gloucestershire GL56 9JY
Tel: 01386 701177
Email: info@ruralretreats.co.uk
Web: www.ruralretreats.co.uk

More adventurous holiday-makers can join *THV Patricia*, the flagship of the Trinity House Fleet, as her crew carry out their vital work of maintaining lighthouses and lightships. For more information, contact Trinity House on:
Tel: 01255 245034
Email: contractual.services@thls.org
Web: www.trinityhouse.biz

For other contacts in the UK and abroad, see:

The National Trust for Scotland Holidays Department
Tel: 0131 243 9331
Email: holidays@nts.org.uk
Web: www.nts.org.uk

The Landmark Trust
Shottesbrooke, Maidenhead,
Berkshire SL6 3S
Tel: 01628 825925
Email: bookings@landmarktrust.org.uk
Web: www.landmarktrust.org.uk

Joy Adcock, of the Association of Lighthouse Keepers, published *Lighthouse Accommodation: Britain and Worldwide* in 2003. This useful guide gives contacts and booking details for accommodation, as well as information on visitor centres and museums in the UK and abroad.
ISBN 0 9535182 1 3

Maritime Heritage

You can use the contacts below as a starting point to explore Britain's outstanding maritime life and history.

For a comprehensive online guide to maritime museums, sites and facilities in the UK, visit the Maritime Britain site:
www.maritimebritain.fsnet.co.uk

The Association of Lighthouse Keepers,
Mike Millichamp, Membership Secretary, 9 Gwel Trencrom, Hayle, Cornwall TR27 6PJ
Web: www.lighthouse.fsnet.co.uk

'Leading Lights' – The International Lighthouse Journal,
Milford Marina, Milford Haven, Pembrokeshire SA73 3AF
Tel: 01646 698825
Fax: 01646 692896
Email: peter.williams@leadinglights.net
Web: www.leadinglights.net

The Lighthouse Society of Great Britain, Gravesend Cottage, Torpoint, Cornwall PL11 2LX
Email: ktrethewey@btinternet.com

World Lighthouse Society,
The Lantern House, 63 Bacton Road, North Walsham, Norfolk NR28 9DS
Tel: 01692 403784
Email: rosalie@davisgibb.fslife.co.uk
Web: www.worldlighthouses.org

The Northern Lighthouse Board (for lighthouses in Scotland and the Isle of Man),
84 George Street,
Edinburgh EH2 3DA
Tel: 0131 473 3100
Fax: 0131 220 2093
Email: enquiries@nlb.org.uk
Web: www.nlb.org.uk

The Commissioners of Irish Lights (for lighthouses throughout Ireland),
16 Lower Pembroke Street,
Dublin 2, Eire
Tel: (00) 353 1 632 1900
Email: info@cil.ie
Web: www.cil.ie

Maritime Heritage Tours,
Michael Walter, Corston House,
56 Spencer Road, Ryde,
Isle of Wight PO33 3AD
Email: m_walters@martours.demon.co.uk

The National Trust owns many sites of interest for lighthouse enthusiasts, including:

The Lizard Wireless Station at Bass Point in south Cornwall, the site of Marconi's historic wireless experiments in 1901.
Tel: 01326 290384
Web: www.lizardwireless.org

The Marconi Centre at Poldhu in south Cornwall, which houses an exhibition funded by the Marconi Company.
Tel: 01326 241656
Web: www.mulliononline.com

Orford Ness National Nature Reserve in Suffolk, a secret military test site from 1913 until the mid-1980s, and home to the most powerful light on the east coast of England.
Tel: 01394 450057
Email: orfordness@nationaltrust.org.uk

South Foreland Lighthouse on the White Cliffs of Dover in Kent, where Michael Faraday experimented with the use of electricity in lighthouses.
Tel: 01304 852463
Email: southforeland@nationaltrust.org.uk

Souter Lighthouse on the north-east coast in Tyne and Wear, the first lighthouse to be lit by electricity
Tel: 01670 773966
Email: souter@nationaltrust.org.uk

The Gribbin Daymark near Fowey in south Cornwall, an 84-foot high tower that visitors can climb on summer Sundays. For opening times, tel: 01208 265235 or 01726 870146.

The information above, which does not represent a comprehensive listing, is accurate at the time of going to press.

Selected Bibliography

Adcock, Joy
Lighthouse Accommodation: Britain and Worldwide (2003)

Armstrong, Richard
Grace Darling – Maid and Myth (1965)

Bathurst, Bella
The lighthouse Stevensons: the extraordinary story of the building of the Scottish lighthouses by the ancestors of Robert Louis Stevenson (1999)

Hague, Douglas
Lighthouses of Wales: Their Architecture and Archaeology (1994)

Hague, Douglas and Christie, Rosemary
Lighthouses: Their Architecture, History and Archaeology (1975)

Hart-Davis, Adam
Henry Winstanley and the Eddystone Lighthouse (2002)

Naish, John
Seamarks: Their History and Development (1985)

Nicholson, Christopher
Rock Lighthouses of Britain (1983)

Williams, Peter
Beacon on the Rock: the dramatic history of lighthouses from Ancient Greece to the present day (c.2001)

Woodman, Richard & Wilson, Jane
The Lighthouses of Trinity House (2002)

Picture Credits

Index

First published in Great Britain in
2005 by National Trust Enterprises
Limited, 36 Queen Anne's Gate,
London SW1H 9AS
www.nationaltrust.org.uk
Registered charity number 205846

ISBN 0 7078 0397 7

Designed by TRUE
Printed and bound in Hong Kong

Front cover: Souter Lighthouse,
Tyne and Wear, photographed in 1992
(NTPL/Matthew Antrobus)

Back cover: Beachy Head Lighthouse,
East Sussex (NTPL/David Sellman)